REFLEXION ON LOSS

Smart Odiase

First published in Great Britain as a softback original in 2024

Copyright © S. O. Odiase

The moral right of this author has been asserted.

All rights reserved.

No part of this publication may be reproduced, stored in a retrieval system, or transmitted, in any form or by any means, without the prior permission in writing of the publisher, nor be otherwise circulated in any form or binding or cover other than that in which it is published and without a similar condition including this condition being imposed on the subsequent purchaser.

TABLE OF CONTENTS

DEDICATION. IV

PREFACE 1

CHAPTER 1
  SOFT SPOT - ACTS. 5

CHAPTER 2
  NATURE OF SOFT SPOT. 13

CHAPTER 3
  CONSEQUENCES OF LOSS. 17

CHAPTER 4
  ELIMINATING LOSS SOFT SPOT 21

CHAPTER 5
  LOSS POLICIES 27

CHAPTER 6
  PROPRIETARY ADVANTAGE. 35

CHAPTER 7
  SECURITY POLICY. 43

CHAPTER 8
  SUMMARY 73

ABOUT THE AUTHOR 75

REFERENCES 77

Dedication

This book is dedicated to my maternal grandparents for their insightful approach that raised me to be contented with whatever I have and never to envy others.

It is also dedicated to my parents who encouraged me to sustain integrity in all life situations.

Finally, it is dedicated to my divinely made and beloved children, and to my amiable wife lady Grace Amenaghawon Odiase. They availed me a blissful retirement environment which enabled the writing of this book.

All honour, glory and adoration with thanksgiving be alone to the Almighty God for the privileged opportunity to write this book. To you O Lord is all glory for the great things you have done for me and my family. Help me to remain faithful to eternity in Jesus' name.

Amen.

Preface

The meaning of Loss in the Cambridge English language Dictionary is that one no longer has something and the Concept Definition is the lack or deprivation of what is owned. The author of this book is keying into the two meanings. The situation might be as not active in right moral as error is now seen in nations / organizations / corporations, people as well as the culprits through undesirable risk response to rules and procedures.

The book of Esther in the holy bible validates it in the lives of Vasti; Haman; and Mordecai during the reign of King Ahasuerus. Queen Vashti lost her evaluation as queen to ESTHER following her disobedience; Haman's inordinate quest for authority resulted in a loss to his family as he was hung in the gallows he prepared for Mordecai.

King Ahasuerus in this scenario had a royal feast for the Nobles in his provinces and at the peak of the event requested to show off the beauty of his Queen Vashti and sent for her to appear in the venue, but she ignored the statement and failed to submit.

The Nobles felt the action of QUEEN VASTI could run viral within their sphere of influence and could make all women defy their husbands. They then passed a judgment that Queen Vashti must free her position for a new queen.

Haman sought to punish Mordecai a Jew for the offense of not bowing to him by eliminating all Jews in the provinces. His appeal got authorization to annihilate all Jews from King Ahusderus whilst the intervention of the new Queen Esther a Jew saw Haman ending up on his gallows.

Nations, corporate organizations, families, and individuals suffer loss in various ways and intensity; without really appreciating underlying explanations.

Some of these reasons are traceable to human acts, nature, and administrative catastrophes. These human acts are born out of disobedience to orders, instructions, or laws, survival instincts due to lack of reward systems, greed, design failures (collapse building and accidental issues)

Some human activities result in environmental penalties like the depreciation of the ozone layer, and other geological acts that root tragedy / destruction.

Though, God's design for mankind is tied up with obedience and orderliness while lawlessness is a tacit choice of human pursuit. The first man Adam was given a code of conduct to manage the earth – "So God created man in his image of God created he him, male and female created them. And God blessed them, and God said unto them, be fruitful, and multiply and replenish the earth, and subdue it; ……. (Gen 1:27-30 KJV)." And as Israel became the chosen nation, Moses was given the Ten Commandments for the nation to follow Exodus 20: 1-20. At the advent of Christ Jesus, He summarized the Ten Commandments into two: "Thou shall love thy God with all thy heart and with all thy soul and with thy mind. And the second 1 is like unto it. Thou shall love thy neighbor as thyself "(Matt 22: 37 -40)

Whilst the apostles and other men of God were inspired by the Holy Spirit to write the words of God for believers to shadow.

These codes of conduct were created to guide against deviation from God's will for man by man. It is a sample for creatures to emulate and imbibe. It is recorded in the holy bible that God used to visit Adam in the cold of the evening to fellowship with Adam.

But man, contention for self-rule inspired tacit disobedience. Israel as a nation were punished when they refused to comply and only pardoned when they repented.

However, due to deviation from godly principles, there are many ungodly activities today going on in a nation and organization that persist and if allowed without check can dehydrate human and material resources to noxious conditions.

People engaged themselves in these objectionable practices due to uncontrolled insatiability / selfishness and weakness in enlightenment or error in patriotism / civic responsibility and communal love. Fatalities are the nuisance of a lack of enforcement of codes of conduct and safety procedures that elicit citizens / personnel positive responses. These incidences persist due to a lack of fear of arrest and appropriate chastisement.

Today the world has become a violent environment and adversity, which is crowded with daily news of horrific incidences of loss of assets through assassination, kidnapping, corruption, and dastard acts. Meanwhile, these horrific incidences are being experienced by nations, corporate bodies, and families.

Nigeria first experienced its first mail bomb assassination of a Chief media executive in 1986 and since then many persons have died from suicide bombings, terrorism, and gunshot assassination whilst kidnapping records abound, these justify the growing need for celebrity, business organizations, high profile individuals and their spouses to uphold the culture of national / organization / family security failure / loss preparedness.

Some records of these security failures / loss of lives include; Mr. Dele Giwa, a media guru who was assassinated via letter bomb inside his home in 1986. Mr. Idah a Local Government Chairman was assassinated at his office in Benin City in 1992. PA Alfred Rewane an opinion leader was assassinated in his home at Ikeja, Lagos. Mrs. Kadrat Abiola a business tycoon and political activist was assassinated being in motion in Lagos. Mr. Hen Shaw a Political leader in his own right was assassinated at home in Abuja. Chief Bola Ige a party-political appointee (Attorney General) was assassinated at his home in Ibadan. Mr. Apata an educationist was assassinated at his home in Isolo, Lagos. Chief Barnabas Igwe the Chairman Onitsha branch Bar Association and his wife Abigail Amaka were assassinated at their home in Onitsha

Recently, there has been suicide improvise explosive devices bombing attacks at embassies, churches, mosques, and market venues in Abuja, Kano, and northern eastern parts of Nigeria. It has become worrisome at the growing insecurity and unprepared state of protection in the nation.

This book enunciates inclusive systems to recognize and thrive the root of doings that cause losses as a response to conscientious supervision. It encourages loyalty awareness and imbibes payback concerns and lawlessness consequence consciousness.

Chapter 1

Soft Spot - Acts

Most people and organizations underestimate the doings that deteriorate positive feelings, thus letting the import of the incidences trigger discontent and avoidable losses to continue with less alarm. These worrying occurrences usually abridge in human retort to behavior and psychosomatic condition / propensity to survival attractiveness.

People get involved in conducts likely to expose nation / organization to both tangible and intangible losses without actually appreciating the danger posed by their action(s) as well as Commission or Omission. Occasionally, this action is driven by the perceived unfairness associated with the guiding system that reflects recompense insufficiency.

Such negative thought fuels the response of a Laissez-fair approach to tasks and conflict of interests counting other factors responsible for loss-induced practices as follows:

ACQUISITIVENESS

Such nature of prey with negative thoughts strong desire for more wealth possessions and powers seem to be the reason for the foolhardy looting of national coffers by some opportunistic management personnel without honour or fear of God in most so-named developing nations.

BAD SYSTEM

Persons whose needs and wants seemingly cannot be met by their legitimate action set on to introduce criminal means as palliative measures to offset them.

LUSTFUL DESIRE

This leads to the manipulation or misrepresentation of statistics / truths or documents to facilitate the illegal acquisition of goods or financial / monetary gains that constitute leakages in a nation and organization.

   a. People's conduct is a response to the mixture of three powerful pushes, namely:

   b. Situational anxiety

   c. Ease of opportunity to commit and conceal crimes.

   d. Justification of the demeanor

These three motivating drives can be illustrated with the three elements of fire origin which are heat, fuel, and oxygen that combine to produce a fire. When only two of the three fire elements are present, a fire cannot happen. Although loss motivating forces, unlike fire, cannot be eliminated completely but can be significantly reduced by supervision to diminish the opportunity to commit and conceal a crime, situational anxiety, and justification of a shameful demeanor.

Dishonest acts will occur when given the right pressures / situational anxiety, and opportunity to commit and conceal crime accompanied by palatable excuse / justification to explain away unprofessional misconducts; most people have the propensity to abuse resources.

The use of official vehicles for personal concern and misuse of corporate special consideration by personnel are common scenes in some intuition yet contribute to an organizational loss. These perceived needs of the possible victims bother on apparent needs that cannot be satisfied within legitimate available resources accessible to the victims at the time the need happens.

SITUATIONAL ANXIETY

This is stirred by external influences on victims due to their elevation in the being of their family members and friends. For instance, a potential victim who is assigned a post of influence while being congratulated is told that he has made it; signifying that the person has reached an affluence status to partake in national / corporate resources. As a result, the individual endures spurious requests / demands from these so-called family members and friends to make the victim cut corners. Including being besieged or told what orders in the same position had realized materially to suggest the victim is timorous for failing to utilize her / his opportunity to misuse workplace resources.

As such psychological tortures on the potential prey accumulate, the person's integrity would be compromised and become victim to corrupt practices and misuse of corporate / national resources while making losses in the organization.

Other elements are:

ELASTICITY

This can be due to addiction to drug and alcohol reliance, gambling, over protracted credit, and peer group pressure with false value orientation contributing factors as well as when employees' financial elasticity reaches its outer limit.

For example, an employee that has a family health issue that requires financial need and has no legitimate ready means but has corporate money that he / she failed to bank on schedule in his / her counter drawer; thus, the victim uses the money to offset the family health bill. If the money were taken to the bank immediately after it was received, the victim would not have had easy access to the money for his / her personal need that demanded urgent care without due process. She / he could see the misconduct as a necessary thing to do to solve family problems and would not feel culpability.

DRUG AND ALCOHOL

Drug and Alcohol Abuse makes the addict seek extra financial resources to procure them for use as the addict can never buy high without them. So, when availed of the opportunity to access resources through illegal means to meet the demand, they go for it headlong; particularly if the addict can explain away the action easily.

PEER GROUP

If one fits into a group of higher taste than one's income, it leads to cutting corners to get ends meet to flow well with the peer group's needs. Another causative factor is unusual employees' lifestyles.

OPPORTUNITIES TO COMMIT AND CONCEAL CRIMES

These modes result from defects in the administrative structure operational procedure that led to crimes in accounting / stock taking within an organization. Also, no one is held responsible for corporate or nationwide sufferers. The underlying belief is anything can happen without fear, disciplinary action, or sanction. This results in the following incidents:

Poor internal control that is the authorization, custody, and accounting procedures being upheld by the same individual (non-segregation of duties) results in a perceived opportunity to commit and conceal crime.

Also, conditions that allow victims of loss propensity to be solely interested in their security reason for the action and not the action or its consequence breed collusion / conspiracy tendencies.

An administration without a built-in mechanism responsible for loss portfolio in an organization as well as fear of victimization to report discovery by a whistle-blower is likely to promote leakages.

POOR STOCK INSPECTION

The under-listed discrepancies create avenues for losses:

Mere counting the number of carton stock faking while neglecting the content at inventory check aids in concealing losses.

Any institution that does not pay attention to unconventionality is likely to suffer losses.

Inadequate sanction of offenders inspires other employees to take.

Improper handling of transaction documents could lead to modification.

Defective hiring system that is poor / lacks of background checks of prospective employees.

Ineffective physical safeguard product and flaw housekeeping and the lack of a formal system for reporting suspicious incidents including lack of anonymity in reporting suspicious incidents promotes losses.

Worker, who draws up a bill, verifies, approves, enters, makes payable, and pays bill.

Creditors are not linked to permanent master data, including an account number. This information must always be entered manually.

Administration works with master data. The person who makes the invoices payable is also authorized to change this master data.

Where there is no adequate inspection of cash flows. Income, expenditure, and bank deposits are either not checked or are not checked sufficiently.

Where there is an unexplainable shrinkage. And an appropriate amount is reserved for this every year. The cause of the shrinkage is rarely investigated.

Employees in the financial administration department can easily take over each other's tasks if one of them is ill and / or on holiday; they are all-rounder.

As soon as an employee receives cash, he passes it on to the accountant without the money being counted and / or a receipt being written out, signed, and recorded.

An employee holds onto cash until he can deposit this cash himself and different records are kept in the cash book.

A situation where there are uncontrolled- receipt / transaction booklets in the accounting department.

To reduce these loopholes, organizations should make staffs aware of how co-worker dishonesty hurts success. The staff needs to recognize that losses take a bite out of everyone's benefits. It can also be reduced with good internal controls and punishment.

JUSTIFICATION OF MISDEMEANOR

This mode is apparent when workers think that it is no longer a crime to do malevolent / shameful acts that cause losses to an organization / community. The workers / national believe it is normal and generate want in doing deprived of thinking of the consequences to the society, or nation.

Rationalization is the cover-up of obvious events of shame with excuses like self-encouraging thoughts like I am / we are not hurting anyone personally by the action. The corporate body does not sufficiently recognize me / us, nor are my / our efforts appreciated by the group. I am / we are sharing out of the profit earned by the group. Everyone does it and it is for a good purpose and not that grave.

Any situation that encourages slogans below among workers breeds losses:

a. It is ours and man must survive.

b. The Boss does it too.

c. I cannot change the situation.

d. It is already a norm.

Chapter 2

Nature Of Soft Spot

Among the components that determine whether a person could be more prone to workplace nonconformity include heredity, socialization, psychology, and mindset.

These are ecological factors that also play a role in contributing to a worker's misconduct such as collective workroom attitude when every worker's action is determined by his or her desire at the expense of corporate interest which is prejudiced by the way the company treats the worker. Illegal access to merchandise and money due to weak control and accounting procedures creates loss potential. Trade confidence exposed to competitors leads to competitive beneficial loss. Poor key administration allows admission to deceit-inclined persons. Authorizations and codes put into the wrong hands can have disastrous effects on a company's assets.

Below are happenings and contributing factors accountable for avoidable losses in an organization, as follows:

1. Laissez-faire ways are put up within the work plan.
2. Mischievous of corporate properties.
3. Unfaithfulness to corporate values and ethics.
4. Intimidation and threats to personnel.
5. Violent agitation.
6. Restiveness.
7. Channeling Materials through third party.
8. Illegal appropriation sum of money.
9. Illegal gathering of corporate information.
10. Faking invoice / voucher, company letter heading, and signature.
11. Gaps in facility administration.
12. Confidence crisis and suspicion.
13. Employees' unpleasant family situations negligence.
14. Fictitious names / parody or reluctance to go or avoidance of leave schedule.
15. Compromising confidential documents / records or Illegal fee collection.
16. Employees' unruly habits.
17. Posting of fictitious credits.
18. Granting undeserved overtime.
19. Merchandizing.
20. Assassination.

21. Product sold with a considerable reduction.

22. Sale without a receipt; Loading without supervision.

23. Loss of a Signed Contract with employment containing a restrained section.

24. Destruction / or loss of 'now' disadvantageous contract agreements.

25. Illegal oil bunkering / smuggling.

26. Diversion of oil tanker or product.

27. Suppression of information on the instrument of payment.

28. Over and under-invoicing.

29. Dereliction of duty.

30. Theft of sensitive / valid product lifting document.

31. Illegal extension of credit facility.

32. Overcomputation of needs / requisition.

33. Unauthorized use of company assets.

34. Abusing employees' privileges / benefits.

35. Conflict of interest.

36. Conspiracy and falsifying billing records on the account of a customer.

37. Forgery and abuse of piracy.

38. Assaulting or harassing employees.

39. Improperly offering, soliciting, or accepting gifts or business courtesies.

40. Working under the influence of any drug and unauthorized possession of firearms or other dangerous weapons in the company's facility.

41. Discriminatory practices with customers.

Chapter 3

Consequences Of Loss

The consequences of loss can be itemized and broken down into the effect on the nation's stability, industry's resilience, and workers / populace as enunciated below.

WORKERS / POPULACE

The employees of an organization prone to leakages inadvertently inflict on themselves the under-mention consequences:

CONFIDENCE CRISIS / SUSPICION

There will be a lack of confidence or increased suspicion within the management and the staff. This lack of trust principals to low productivity and income to the organization thereby decreasing the dispensable income to run the organization and other corporate promises.

LOOSE BENEFITS

The workers' corporate benefits will either be reduced or totally removed, and salaries / wages become Irregular and / or accumulated arrears of payment. This situation makes the workers lose control of their homes they can no longer meet their family commitments due to lack of financial authority at home.

LOW MORALE

The workers will be edgy, causing more insecurity with low morale. The organization then needs more security cost investment. Frustration leads to increased survival instinct and crime rate.

LAY OFF

As the organization develops penniless the business crinkles up and the laborers are thrown into the labor market, all due to self-inflicted consequences of uncontrolled wish to cut corner

CORPORATION

The consequences of uncontrolled loss of business revenue are underscored as follows:

Low productivity means less income to run the organization which results in overhead cuts and subsequent discounts of workers (Right sizing, Salary irregular or not being paid)

Welfare schemes become unachievable and lead to low morale in the labor force therefore customers' demands will not be met, resulting in customers' disaffection and depleted profit.

INCREASE IN SECURITY COST

Investment in providing security will be skewed and insufficient revenue accruing lead to the company becoming bankrupt and folding up.

NATION

The effect of uncontrolled leakages in a nation has great damage to the citizens' wellbeing, and national developments which manifest as follows:

DEPLETE REVENUE

As the countrywide resources are depleted by corruption and then leaks, the national treasure becomes inadequate to meet the nation's planned development. This is characterized by abandoned projects; the administration will start projects that cannot be finished due to insufficient funding and poor infrastructures such as bad road ecological malfunctions. social amenities such as power, and health services cannot be accessed by a lower squad of populace and so disgruntled Citizens.

POLITICAL INSTABILITY

Unemployment is caused by an inability to pay workers as at when due breed strikes by Labour unions and the opportunity for criminals to usurp any peaceful protest to unlatch mayhem on innocent citizens resulting in violent crimes, illegal arms acquisition, and terrorism which create uncertainty and increase security cost in the climate of poor revenue.

RIGHT SIZING

When the nation is not able to pay workers' salaries, it will consider downing its labor force which enhances unrest and tends to reduce the political will to decide by the government.

INVESTORS

In such a state investor consider the removal of their business to a more promising location. Foreign loan conditionality's become the bay out choice for a fire brigade eventuality.

Chapter 4

Eliminating Loss Soft Spot

It is worthy to state that if soft spot incidences are brought to an end or rejected in an organization; it would greatly improve corporate profit margin, good governance, enhanced welfare scheme, and avert leak openings.

To cancel such an incident requires a corporate program that is well understood by all and sundry that delineates corporate view and action to stamp out leak openings in the organization. Such a program must be comprehensive and dutifully moralized to all employees at the different opportunities.

The program implementation must elicit fear of being exposed and ultimate discipline in all staff and no sacred cow. That is the fear of being caught must be obvious in the administrative guidelines for business performance which cause compliance in the direction of the corporate ethics and policy.

Company efforts to remedy losses arising from workers' habits hinge on promulgating policies that will reduce the consequence of the key factors of pressure, opportunity to steal, and probable justification of their loss upbringing habits. This is putting in place policies, procedures, and reward systems that can ameliorate the effect of pressure, opportunity, and justification (which are the elements that make the victim believe in their actions that lead to corporate losses as a fair deal). Loss prevention has both illegal and administrative sanctions. The fertile soil for losses in an organization is weak administrative sanction which tolerates a relatively high level of corporate losses.

It is a good business practice to have standards and procedures for operating a business agenda. These practices and standards are usually embodied in the company's Business Procedure Manual (standard operating procedure).

A company without such a manual stands the risk of heavy losses in terms of money and materials to lustful employees and fraudsters. If the trend of corporate losses is not arrested, it can liquidate a company. So, a company wishing to remain in business for long must have formal written procedures and practices that guide all the employees in their day-to-day conduct of the company's business.

Good employee relation and clear instructions from supervisors reduces the risk of theft and cutting corners.

Management staff must also set an example by adhering to policies and making staff aware of the benefit of consistent operations. Values, simplify the choice-making process and always allow fraud to be prevented or detected on time.

As new staff are taken on board after employment due process, it is mandatory to review the current practices and procedures with them.

It is recommended here that organizations make workers and their basic needs the thrust of the corporate welfare package. Interview staff at the point of separation helps the corporate body to have comments on its operating procedures and / or administrative model.

Holding formal and informal forums to explain corporate strategies, procedures, corporate values and interests to staff and workers is essential to loss prevention explanation.

Business's first line of prevention is contented staff this can be achieved by involving them in the process of creating solutions and mobilizing their consent to internalize solutions.

It is management accountability to maintain a vigilant posture in safeguarding the company's assets and revenues which include computer time, data soft-ware, hardware, programs, and fixed and other movable resources.

Management attitude towards security must always reproduce a positive approach to motivate subordinates to take a similar positive approach whenever they are obligated to discharge their security responsibilities. If management staff submit themselves to security procedures such temperament spurs security detail to exercise their function without fear or favor to all workers and visitors.

Staff must understand that controls are being upheld and strong measures will be taken against people who do not cooperate in helping to maintain those levels of security. Workers must know why rules exist; and that rules are enforced, and they must know what to do

The corporate body should develop loss prevention training programs including three security awareness practices, namely:

A. BRAINWASHING

New staff should have an overview of corporate security and norms before they are assigned responsibility. The purpose of employee orientation is to ensure that new personnel understand the security standards and the role they are expected to play in loss prevention in corporate Facilities.

A successful Orientation will stimulate questions, provide a comfortable setting for reflecting potentially sensitive issues, and clearly demonstrate that loss prevention is a high priority in the group. Documents of this meeting give management tangible proof that it has taken the initiative to ensure that standards and responsibilities have been taught and understood.

This awareness program is for all newly hired employees (full-time, part-time, and Temporary), including all transferring employees who have not been Oriented previously or do not have it noted in their personal files (includes all employees, irrespective of position – for example, Sales, management. etc.).

It is at this review the new staff are informed of the zero tolerance to induced corporate loss, the welfare packages, and the reward system.

B. REF-BRIEFING

During service, there should be a regular review of corporate security policy and loss prevention regulations to keep them abreast with corporate procedures and norms and workers informed of the publication of loss prevention awardees if security policy permits doing so. Throughout the re-briefing efforts will be made to request participants for their contribution to enhance loss prevention programmes and symbols. Staff forum enhances the involvement of the idea of a loss alertness project. Such a forum makes employees imbibe the culture of alertness by being empathetic in their duty and what to do to prevent loss or fraud and willing to react to violations of fraud or loss prevention procedures.

Must ensure that all employees report immediately to their supervisor, manager, coordinator of security, or managing director any suspected or known violation of standards and values.

C. SEPARATION BRIEFS

Management must put in place procedures that enforce at the end of service personnel interview to have an insight into his / her after-service plan and any corporate grievances or thoughts if any.

Chapter 5

Loss Policies

The business body will silhouette typical trace hostile toward corporate worth to set normal to follow by the choice panel for prospective applicant meeting. What is more, standard procedure that exposes unacceptable does in the company must be in the company manual.

Management orders disciplinary processes / procedures whilst breaches of internal control measures by employees must be uniformly sanctioned to serve as a deterrent to others.

There should be induced discipline in the work force and uphold ethical standards. Institute a broadminded record system and performance measurement standard to motivate employees.

A system to carry out periodic updates of operational procedures to match development is in action. And create guidelines that spur guiding capability and encourage consistency in the application of sanctions for violations of prescribed codes.

Formulate and implement robust information security policies and contingency plans. Employee training and development must be relevant and reliable to enhance in-house capability.

Institute an employee's support system to enhance workers' standard of living and institute loss prevention alertness policies realization project.

Enhance investment in communication infrastructure to avoid extended down time, which makes control breaks.

The organization's work ethics must be relevant to workers' requirements and aspirations.

The program designed for loss reduction must make use of a variety of signs / decals that can be attached in high – traffic, high-visibility areas in and around the facility as well as on perimeter fencing, company vehicles, contract vehicles, etc.

The location security Manager should check and replace signage on an as-needed basis. A key part of the program involves periodic distribution of educational awareness materials such as posters, flyers, etc.

As the program matures, new materials and events will be developed and provided to location security coordinators, along with any necessary instructions such as If you have an idea or a need for additional support materials for the awareness program, please contact your Security Manager or corporate security Head.

To curtail conflict of interest in doing company business it is necessary to codify all employees' conduct in their assigned responsibility and to conduct personal business on the highest ethnical level. No other activities must conflict with the corporate best interest.

Each employee is obliged to remain alert to potential situations. Those questions not clearly answered in the guidelines should be directed to the worker's supervisors or the security executive.

Below are suggested guidelines for the corporate employment model:

Staff may not own any properties or interests in an organization that would result in a conflict with the interest of the employer.

Workers may not release directly or indirectly any data relating to competitive bids submitted by or to the business, to anyone outside or to anyone within not having a business need-to-know. Staff may not disclose proprietary or confidential information regarding plans, financial data, clientele, or any other information that could be detrimental to it.

Personnel may discuss proprietary information with persons doing business with it when that information is essential to the business at hand. In this case, the employee must record the nature of the information and the method of disclosure.

Workforces shall not seek or accept personal gain directly or indirectly from anyone soliciting business or doing business with it or from any competitor.

Examples of such personal gain are gifts, gratuities, favors, loans, guarantees of loans, excessive entertainment, and rewards.

However, a company must recognize acceptance of certain courtesies of nominal value that will not adversely affect its best interest.

Other than the common business courtesies mentioned previously, an employee will not offer or provide personal gain to any one or to any organization seeking to influence a business relationship with the company.

Staff may not participate in any outside employment, self-employment, or vocation or serve as officers, directors, partners, or consultants for outside organizations. If such activity reduces work efficiency, interferes with the ability of the employee to act conscientiously, properly, or confidential procedures, plans, or techniques.

Workers who inadvertently find out their objectivity may be questioned because of individual interests or family or personal relationships should immediately consult with their supervisor.

Individual managers and employees are responsible for the protection of assets under their supervision, control, and use.

Protection of life, property, and assets is a key element of sound management and practice.

Each facility location is responsible for developing a comprehensive security program.

All losses with security implications involving property or personnel will be investigated.

Company will in appropriate circumstances, report to public security authorities apparent violations of criminal Law concerning personnel, property, or proprietary information.

Businesses will regularly audit the security programs to assist managers in, complying with all aspects of the program that they have developed or for which they have responsibility.

The corporate organization must streamline its worrisome and unacceptable incidences that the company orders total adherence to the corporate vision statement. Those activities which promote loss are the objective of corporate loss prevention preparedness. An organization considers the incidents unacceptable because they have negative impacts on the success or safety of the company, employees, or customers.

These unacceptable acts should be addressed in an open, straight forward manner because, in far too many cases, these activities do occur simply because someone is not adequately informed.

Workers must understand that the company feels strongly about no adherence, as it is a basic responsibility to clearly and continually communicate to them exactly what is expected of them. This helps them to avoid errors in judgments and the consequences.

The policy makes stipulation anyone that who has a question concerning the suitability of any consideration should discuss it with his / her supervisor before he or she acts.

The corporate organization must have written terms and conditions of service that itemize what and how to guide and regulate human resource staff's responsibilities and duties, such as vision and goal of the organization; hiring and firing policies, promotion, aids, correction. This will put the employee and management on the same page though the synergy of standard operation procedures in action will prevent loss of man hours and enhance harmony in the establishment.

People who play an important role in corporate loss avoidance policy are customers, suppliers, and neighbors. Separately, these groups have the potential to prevent losses. When they are participants in the program awareness of loss prevention, encourages them to become involved in it.

Such polices generate positive involvement by staff, customers, and suppliers. It thus provides measures to determine the effectiveness of loss incident prevention and to recognize those who take prevention action. it is vitally important to document involvement whenever possible.

Decals and other signage will convert customers, and suppliers into a prevention resource. Direct communication with this group will further increase their awareness and make it even easier for them to become involved in loss prevention efforts.

Here are general ideas for making customers, and suppliers, part of the loss prevention program:

An announcement letter could be sent to each customer, and supplier shortly after the program has been introduced in the locations.

A similarly worded letter could be incorporated with invoices and shipments to customers and in cheques to suppliers.

An annual announcement could be sent to customers and suppliers, which focuses on corporate Gifts and business courtesy policy.

RECOGNITION OF OUTSTANDING INVOLVEMENT

When someone shares an idea or concern that helps prevent a loss, it is noted and kept in the recognition of outstanding involvement in loss prevention files.

If an employee brings security vulnerability such as an unlocked door or a suspicious person in the parking lot to the attention of management, he / she should be recognized. If an employee shares a concern regarding actual abuse such as threats harassment or other violations of company Standards, it should also be documented.

The security executive and location management must use discretion based on the nature of the information provided. There may be cases where documentation and recognition of involvement need to be handled in a very confidential manner.

Such recognition letter / announcement must be treated with caution whilst a copy is sent to the corporate security head and originally kept in the personnel record.

The document is used in a positive manner to recognize top performers individually and their facilities. Recognition can be as simple as a letter from the appropriate cooperate or Division manager. In addition, facility management should recognize the individual so that the person's supports are appreciated.

One way to communicate loss prevention deterrent programs effectively in a single or Multi-store retail environment is through a loss prevention bulletin. A bulletin can serve several functions in minimizing employee theft. For example, if the publication prints audit scores, managers will know that the company is actively monitoring the control of these areas and that the scores are taken seriously. In addition, a loss prevention manager may want to publicize the best and the worst cash-handling personnel in the store.

The scores that will be listed are the total amount of cash overages and shortages and the total number of voids. This is an excellent opportunity to publicly reward those employees who are handling cash properly and to identify employees who may need retraining. Tracking employee's cash averages and shortages is critical in daily business and maintaining profit.

Chapter 6

Proprietary Advantage

PHYSICAL SECURITY

Preparing for proprietary advantage involves pain pain-taken arrangements necessary to prevent assessed security breaches threat techniques and to reduce related threats.

Physical security is that part of security that concerns physical obstacles disposed of in-depth to frustrate the attacks of spies and saboteurs. Physical security measures are based on the principles of protection in depth working from the likely target of attack towards the boundary. An investigation has led to the conclusion that nothing is more important to effective security than the basic measures of physical security if well planned and consistently carried out.

Security controls are a combination of rules and Instruction; physical measures and Screening / vetting of personnel. Thus Security Managers must realize, however, that physical obstacles are not a complete substitute for personnel. No physical security measures have yet been devised which cannot be surmounted by an attacker who has the necessary skill and time.

The main function of physical obstacles is "to buy time" and a protective device can only be relied on for the time it takes to surmount it.

Physical security procedures must complement rules and education including the screening of people who have authorized access to sensitive materials and specially sensitive installations. They cannot be applied without security education and training, constant vigilance, and careful planning.

The evaluated target to be protected must first be defined and then concentrated in a few locations after the threat has been assessed. The time estimated to surmount physical security procedures is usually related to the weakest point in the chain of protection.

PERIMETER FENCE

documents and other valuables

It is important to note that protective elements of proprietary advantage are assembled from the targets towards the perimeter fence.

The outer rectangular wall of protection represents a perimeter fence and security lighting.

The second rectangular wall of protection represents security guards' responsibilities and guard dogs.

The third rectangular wall of defense represents security permits / ID cards / permits and other security regulator measures.

The fourth rectangular wall of protection represents security strategies and security procedure guidelines.

The fifth rectangular wall of protection represents a physical safeguard, segregated proprietary assets.

The Centre's rectangular wall of protection represents a strong room, security locks, and security containers housing documents and other valuables.

PROP UP PROPRIETARY ADVANTAGE

The protection of proprietary advantage is the technique of ensuring that commercial trade secrets, product engineering, and vital documents do not get into the wrong hands by controlling access to them as follows:

Need to know demand that circulation of sensitive information should be kept to an absolute minimum. No person should be given more information than is necessary to enable him / her to carry out his / her duties efficiently.

The permission of access is determined by the duty schedule, it is important to note that a vetting or background clearance confers no automatic right to sight sensitive information or grade information.

Need to hold denotes that a person may need to see the contents of a particular graded sensitive information, but it does not necessarily follow that he / she has to hold the document in any form.

Persons should therefore be permitted to hold only sensitive information which is essential to the performance of their responsibilities this is carried out by a password / code system.

Need to take proposes the fact that a person may need to see the contents of a sensitive document and indeed have a need to hold that document but only in circumstances where the need can be shown to be real can the document be removed from the office.

If such a document is removed from its filing cabinet; the person must accord the document adequate protection and care.

HOW TO PREPARE PROPRIETARY DOCUMENT

Business organizations must have rules to regulate the production, circulation, and custody of their document in order to protect the document against spies and mole's actions that could result in loss and compromise as follows:

Branded document has to be correctly graded in accordance with the harm unauthorized disclosure would cause the organization that is the document / information sensitivity.

The production of sensitive information as a matter of principle should be limited to a minimum requirement and must be easily traceable.

Highly classified documents should have routine checks and such checks should include losses or modifications.

The storage routine must prevent compromise and easily expose unauthorized access.

Sensitive information / documents should be graded to show the degree of protection required for it and appropriately marked to designate the damage caused by its unauthorized disclosure, misuse theft, or modification.

There are four types of classifications namely:

a. Highly restricted distribution of information that provides a business enterprise, a very major advantage over its competitors or, its misuse or unauthorized disclosure or modification would erode competitive advantage or have severe adverse effects on personnel.

b. The Limited Availability of information provides a business enterprise an advantage over its contestants, or its misuse or illegal revelation theft or alteration would have a noteworthy opposing effect on business activity or personnel.

c. The General Branded Information is information of such a nature that its misuse, illegal disclosure, or alteration would have a partial adverse effect on business activities or personnel.

d. The General Information is information of such a nature that its misuse, illegal disclosure, or alteration would have no adverse effect on business activities or personnel.

CARE OF DOCUMENTS

Documents should be downgraded periodically to allow adequate and reasonable protection in storage. The degree of protection given to a document is in direct relationship with its security grading including File copies, Flash and CDs, Drafts, Stencils, and Spoiled copies.

The use of copy numbers and page numbers such as copy no. 2 of 10, paged 1 of 4, and stapling of documents are essential elements to control documents.

Waste destruction and the use of security containers are recommended for effective protection.

Access to sensitive documents must be limited to those who have been screened and who need to see its contents to carry out their duties.

This is achieved by screening personnel and access control by the document system manager / Administrator. Personnel involved in sensitive records should be segregated from other workforce.

The number of sensitive resources in circulation must be limited as much as possible. All spare copies should be destroyed. The use of distribution lists to control the production of copies of documents is needful. There should be checks of sensitive documents at regular intervals.

Sensitive documents should be securely stored when not in actual use using adequate security containers whilst control of admission to sensitive areas by maintenance staff and cleaners should be under strict control.

There should be no removal of sensitive documents to houses and clubs and during temporary vacation of office, all documents should be kept under lock.

Sensitive documents should be transmitted by secured means using Courier service and Screening of courier personnel. A receipt system for acknowledgment should be enforced.

When a classified document is no longer required, it shall be destroyed by "Weeding" programs destruction by burning and should synchronize with document registers by crossing out any destroyed document from the register.

When the content of a high-grade document becomes less harmful the document should be downgraded. Down grading procedure strikes off the old grading mark and incites the new one including reconciliation to documents registers.

Automatic down grading is enforced by including (This document is to be downgraded to class 3 on first February, 20.... and Inform all concerned of down grading) on the document so produced.

When sensitive documents cannot be found or are alleged to have been compromised, an inquiry should take place and counter-compromise action instituted. The action to nullify the danger is taken to counter the compromise effect.

The staff handling or using delicate information must be trained and exercised on the rules overriding corporate sensitive documents regularly.

PROPRIETARY SECURITY MEASURES

There are no complete resistant security measures governing the internal protective arrangements for all occupants and assets that can be laid down here, but the following suggestions should be adopted to meet the differing needs:

If sensitive documents are not protected in locked security ampules during working hours, it is the responsibility of individual officers and supervisors in large units to ensure that the records cannot be glanced at, handled, or removed by persons -whether employees or visitors who are not authorized to see them.

Documents, which should not be seen by anyone else with access to a room, should be locked up whenever they are not in actual use.

If a room is to be left unoccupied even for a few moments during working hours and it is unrealistic to put the documents away, the door of the room must be locked.

For longer absences, documents must be locked away in security containers.

All rooms must be checked by occupants at the close of work to ensure that all sensitive material and documents including waste have been locked away in security containers.

The containers have been properly locked, and all security keys mustered.

Much can be done to increase security at the workplace by reducing to a minimum the extent to which visitors penetrate the premises.

Control of entry of buildings is best achieved by admitting visitors and staff through only one entrance on a recognition or pass system.

All Security guard posts should have precise written instructions about their duties and should be responsible to the Corporate Security Officer for the efficient performance of their duties. They must feel sure of guidance and support in discharging their duties.

The office or facility is one of the vulnerable point areas where an executive can be attacked hence there should be a mail screening machine to prevent the introduction of an improvise explosive device received through the mail and have external armed guards to deny unauthorized access.

Ideally, the executive's desk should not be placed near windows.

As a routine security procedure, every employee having access to sensitive areas and information must have his / her background investigation conducted on employment to prevent leaks of information and sabotage.

Chapter 7

Security Policy

Physical safeguard measures must be adequate to limit opportunities and reduce temptation. The need to control access to perimeter doors continuously including the receiving door is critical. Many companies have twenty-four-hour alarm protection on these doors to ensure daytime protection, but not all companies consider such extended alarm service cost-effective.

Door seals are recommended for exits that are unprotected during the day, a door seal can be useful in controlling access to the receiving door. Management keeps a door access log recording the date, time, and reason the door is being opened; the old seal number; the replacement seal number, and the person gaining entry.

Merchandise controls should be focused on worker procurements. Staff make buying with their member of staff discount and leave their shopping bags in staff rooms, locker rooms, or workstations, providing an opportunity for other stock to be put in these bags. To deter potential merchandise theft, management should conduct random package checks as staff leave the edifice.

The use of a vendor check-in procedure is another merchandise control program that can be used to minimize internal theft. Outside vendors who come into stores every day are not technically store employees, but they do work for the store and are in unauthorized areas handling merchandise. Vendors are generally accountable for visiting a store consistently, reviewing their own product lines, making essential merchandise vicissitudes, or insertion new orders.

With a vendor checkered-in program, the vendor checks in at a designated place and signs in on a vendor log. The log should contain the date and time of the vendor visit, the vendor's name, the name of the company he or she represents, and the purpose of the visit. The vendor should then be given a vendor badge that is to be worn in the store with his or her name and the company's name. When leaving, the vendor should be required to check in with a designated number of staff who will open the briefcase or boxes that the vendor is taking out of the store.

The counseling process is used to discuss with employees retraining needs and necessary disciplinary action. The loss prevention department should be an advocate of the need to address poor employee cash control. Worker counseling must be conducted as soon as a tricky is noticed. Guidance given as part of the program should be consistent with company policy and all counseling must be documented and signed by the employee.

A loss prevention portfolio should consider how to deal with employee problems; it should consider the following question: is there a written policy or procedure in place addressing employee violation? Is there an employee acknowledgment form stating the policy and signed by the employee? Was the employee professionally trained for his or her responsibilities? Was cash violation properly and thoroughly investigated? After these issues have been addressed; progressive employee counseling can prove to be a useful deterrent to employee dishonesty.

The ability to provide a total deterrent program that involves management and staff will clearly demonstrate a team environment. Empowering employees to recognize the impact of employee theft will enhance loss prevention consciousness and give everyone a sense of responsibility.

In addition, internal controls maintained by management and employees at all levels are designed to prevent actions detrimental to the company's best interest. There are also actions exhibited by corporate employees that seem norm which are harmful and impact corporate profits; these are unauthorized use or misappropriate use of corporate resources (such as stationeries, vehicles, data, equipment, etc.).

Physical security procedures that are enforced by the security department / unit contribute to effectively precluding the removal of movable company properties.

The weakest area of any security plan is the human factor. Time and time again, security breaches occur because internal employees are not security-minded and actively engaged in their own expediency, neglecting the protection of their source of income which is the workplace.

In general, these breaches come in the form of people inadvertently or intentionally overriding security procedures. A typical example of this is that employees typically view the security of the workplace as the company's responsibility therefore they are less mindful of security-related issues and are less alert to security-related problems.

An employee swipes their badge for a friend or a visitor because security measures are perceived as a hassle to go through the security system to collect a visitor badge and / or escort.

Sometimes visitors also can talk their way into the facility past the receptionist, security guard, or other employees which includes some management staff.

These human factors frustrate security operatives and lend room for most security breaches in an organization that breed losses.

Physical security breaches include holes in a fence, doors left open, broken locks, inadequate lighting, and suspicious individuals' functioning.

It is important to be acquainted with the fact that the level of security effectiveness is a function of expression of the worker involved in the program understanding and accepting the significance of the benefits to them in their following the security procedure.

This is done by developing security awareness of incidents specific actions, procedures, and physical security for worst cases scenarios. Compliance with security rules can reduce the potential for personal / personnel injury, property damage, espionage, and business disruption / and enhance business recovery.

PERIMETER FENCES

The perimeter fence can be opaque or transparent; Opaque fences are solid and cannot be seen from outside is that the disadvantage if crime is being committed within the fence people outside cannot deter the criminal that had succeeded in gaining access into the facility. These can be brick walls or other materials. Transparent fences allow people outside the perimeter fence to watch activities happening within it.

The perimeter fence is the first line of protection for assets in depth. This first line of security protection and safeguarding property is a physical barrier. These are fences in conjunction with access control to reduce risk, secure the environment, and reduce liability costs.

A fence can only reduce or delay intrusion, reduce the opportunity for crime, and make the property pleasing. Openings in the periphery of the fence must be kept to a minimum, when necessary, to have an opening. Such openings should be protected or secured. If gates are installed, they should be locked but make sure the gates can be opened in case of emergency or connected to the fire system.

A physical barrier is anything that prevents, hinders, or controls progress or movement. It could be natural, structural, animal, human, or energy. Some of the natural barriers are rivers, cliffs, canyons, seas, etc whilst Structural barriers include fences, walls, floors, grilles, roofs, bars, barbed wires, etc.

The surveyed field (surveillance zone) should extend outside the fence for a minimum distance of twenty meters, preferably fifty meters, and should be reasonably flat and level. It must be clear of obstruction, trees, vegetation, or indeed anything else that could conceal a person viewed from within the defended area.

When the space outside the perimeter fence is very restricted or substantially less than twenty meters or unavoidably obstructed to the extent that it contains a man cover, it may be necessary to employ a double force line.

When the perimeter fencing and patrolling are effective the risk of perpetration by a surreptitious attack on the perimeter will be greatly reduced. A well-defended fence line may daunt the intending intruder, who may then decide that it will be less risky to get inside the site through a legitimate entrance perhaps by using a trick. Similarly, a strong perimeter protection may deter a dishonest employee from attempting to remove goods illegally from the site over the fence, and he may decide to try and bring stolen goods out through the gate. Indeed, the stronger the perimeter, the greater the importance of suitable gate routines and equipment.

Perimeter fences can be enhanced with electric cable and or sensor devices that could deter would-be intruders. Also, trained dogs can keep watch over perimeter fences with or without handlers nearby. Security guards can be employed to watch for breaches or those scalars of perimeter fence.

SECURITY LIGHTING

Almost any kind of exterior lighting will enhance the night security of premises, but lighting that is designed primarily to deter intrusion or night attack will perform this function better. Also, the desired results may be achieved at lower capital costs and with greater responsibility.

Security lighting is provided to aid the protection of premises, property, and persons against night attack; such an attack may be the entry or attempted entry into the protected area by criminal or other disruptive or destructive act.

It is important to recognize that security lighting is a means of crime prevention differing greatly from other security measures like intrusion alarms, closed-loop television, etc., which are mainly methods of crime detection.

The objectives are to prevent the crime from occurring by deterring the criminal, to reveal the criminal before, during, and after his act of intrusion, and to provide the guards with a measure of concealment, so the intruder does not know their number, their activity at any moment, nor if he had been observed by them.

The first objective is achieved largely because of the efficiency with which the second two are achieved, coupled with a deliberate fashioning of the lighting and other protection to make it obvious to the intending intruder that the crime will be difficult to perform undetected. If seen, he may be apprehended, if not apprehended, he may be recognized if known to the guards or may be identified later.

Security guard feels safe with a suitable security lighting system. As a result, guards may patrol more frequently, and more thoroughly, thereby reducing further the risk of intrusion, as well as lessening the possibility of a fire going undetected on the premises.

If no security lighting is provided, the guard will probably patrol with a torch in his hand. This has the following disadvantages:

The guard will spend time between the patrols in a lighted guard house, and thus his vision will be light-adopted. When he steps outside to patrol, it will take some time before he can see very much in the poor light condition. But a criminal outside will be able to see far better, being fully dark-adapted to a low light level.

While patrolling with the torch, the guards' point of visual attention will center on the bright patch cast by the torch. He will adapt to the brightness of the bright patch, and this will delay or prevent his becoming dark-adapted. As a result, his contrast sensitivity will be reduced due to a glare effect, and it is then unlikely that he will become aware of a dark-clothed person standing quietly in the shadows, indeed, he would have a better chance of seeing a low contrast object had he not used the torch at all, but had had sufficient time to become dark-adapted or had been continuously out-doors and not subjected to the bright conditions within the guard house.

A suitable design for security lighting can be formulated using the five basic techniques of security lighting: Perimeter lighting; Check point lighting; Area lighting Floor lighting and Topping-up.

The objectives of the lighting system associated with a check point are:

a. To provide sufficient light inside the house to enable the guard to refer to telephone directories, etc.

b. To use the phone and study documents handed in for confirmation.

c. This lighting should not reveal to anyone outside the guard house the number or activity of the occupants, nor should it handicap the guards from seeing out of windows and affecting vigilant supervision of what occurs outside, nor should it give the occupants and adaptation level differing greatly from that required for efficient vision when they step outside the guard house.

d. To provide sufficient and suitable lighting outdoors in the checkpoint area to enable vehicles and persons to be inspected and searched efficiently and for documents to be checked, and in conjunction with fencing and gating, the lighting should ensure there is no way of anyone slipping past the guard into or out of the premises.

ROLE OF SECURITY GUARDS

Security guards' services are a system of assets / property protection, therefore the role of security guards whether proprietary (personnel of the organization) or contract (personnel of private guard company) is primarily to prevent losses that may occur through crime, fire, and laxity that will affect productivity and consequence profit.

a. Therefore, the approach of security guards is:

b. To prevent things from going wrong

c. To detect anything that might go wrong.

d. To correct anything that goes wrong.

e. To report all things that happen to the organization.

This approach of security guards deters insecurity situations and protects assets while enforcing corporate regulations and standards.

Security guards' everyday jobs include these under-mentioned activities:

a. Keeping watch over key and vulnerable areas in the facility

b. Monitoring access control system

c. Guard house duties

d. Enforcing corporate Standard Operating Procedures

e. Post log and incidence reports

f. Escort visitors within the complex and take messages.

g. Respond to an abnormal occurrence.

h. Negotiate with violators and effect crisis resolution.

i. Act under pressure in times of crisis

j. Secure and maintain lost and found items log / book.

k. Relieve his or her colleagues.

l. Open and close gates

m. Work both day and night

n. Use specialized equipment.

o. Receive parcels or goods after work hours.

POST'S DUTIES

a. Tracking asset

b. Custody of keys movement

c. Static surveillance

d. Staff movement and attendance records

e. Security reports

f. Monitoring both main and alternate facility sources of power

g. Track vehicle movement and goods

h. Take over and hand over procedure.

i. Maintain an incident and occurrence logbook.

j. Response to sensors' sound alarms

k. Maintains Loss and found items record.

l. Response and rehearse contingency plan.

m. Human and traffic control.

TASK OF SECURITY GUARDS

a. Control of access to building premises

b. Patrol of corporate premises

c. Inspection of premises

d. Use of fire extinguishers.

e. Preliminary investigation

f. CCTV and Alarm system supervision

g. Escort duties

h. Manning check points observation and guard post

i. Communication

j. Emergency activities / duties

k. Prevention and detection of crime

l. Protection of Assets

DAILY OCCURRENCES RECORD

Serial Numbers	Date	Time	Particulars	Action Taken	

ACCESS CONTROL DUTIES

a. Checking and verifying the identity of persons entering the premises

b. Documentation of entrants into and those exiting the premises.

c. Searching (if authorized by management rules)

d. Key control (no staff should leave the client's premises with official keys)

e. Dealing with lost and found items.

f. Keeping doors closed always.

g. Directing visitors to points of visit

SECURITY GUARDS AS IMAGE MAKER

Security guards are the first persons a visitor to an organization meets, so security guards' appearance presents the first image of the facility to visitors. Thus, security guards should:

a. Be smart both in dressing and disposition.

b. Give a genuine impression of being capable and efficient.

c. Be friendly to everybody, but familiar with none.

d. Helpful but cautious of ethics

e. Polite but firm in regulation enforcement.

f. He should show respect to everyone without compromising his professionalism.

REPORT WRITING

a. Keep the report short and simple.

b. Do not use big English or slang.

c. Do not delay writing the report.

d. Address the report to the person who will take action promptly.'

The report is meant to provide a source of subsequent reference for any significant details arising from such information or incidents for subsequent reports.

a. To record matters which cannot be safely entrusted to memory.

b. Make these entries at the actual time of the incident or as soon after as possible.

c. Do not erase anything, just cross through mistakes.

d. Do not leave any blank spaces, and do not tear any pages out.

GUARD DOG - DETERRENT AGAINST INTRUDER AND VANDALS

SECURITY DOGS WITH HANDLERS

Shows controlled aggression- Security dog patrol

Security dogs are used as investigation tools and deterrence to would-be criminals. They are apt for crowd control; Static site guarding; Drug detection service; Explosive detection service; Building sites and secure compounds. The handlers are trained in their insinuation (innuendo).

INFORMATION COLLECTION RESPONSIBILITY

Security guards should be guided by instruction on what is required of their function as eyes and ears of the management and to turn in reports that would assist the corporation:

a. Gathering information that will support facility security.

b. Conduct day and night patrol on foot within the facility and observe the absent of the normal or the present of the abnormal

c. Mounting static observation posts and ground surveillance

d. Filing in reports on detected criminals / vandals' activities

e. Transfer of arrested person to the police as per laid down procedure.

f. Report on location and identification of trespasses

g. Protect and monitor sensors.

h. Logistic support to the facility manager

i. Carryout day and Night vehicular (mobile) patrol

j. Intervention operations

k. Create and maintain records for future reference.

l. Liaison with Local Communities

m. Protect and monitor sensors.

n. Security Intelligence acquisition, processing, and dissemination

o. Liaison with security agencies

p. Handle and process suspects

q. Liaison with facilities and other interest groups

SECURITY PROCEDURES IN CORPORATE ORGANIZATION

The primary purpose of every commercial organization is to make a profit and ensure the welfare and security of its employees. Profit can only be made if the organization's asset which includes commercial trade secrets or employees is protected and controlled properly.

The executive officers of an organization are susceptible to attack due to the key roles they play in corporate organizations, so easy access to them must be denied to unscheduled visitors.

The receptionist's manner and orientation on how to receive all visitors and determine their purpose and the worker they want to see must be synchronized to limit the capability of adversaries. He / she should have a panic alarm connecting the position and the chief executive's office to alert him or her in the event of an emergency.

The chief executive office should be paged with an electrically controlled lock or cipher lock and should have curtains or Venetian shades to chunk hostile surveillance whilst the CEO monitors the reception room electronically from the chief executive desk.

All visitors should be subjected to handbag, briefcase, and package screening prior to being permitted access to the executive suite as security protocol. Unexpected visitors may be denied access to the executive's suite. The executive should ensure that his or her secretary does not provide the Boss's home address or telephone number to unknown or unlawful people. The director's secretary must always know the Boss' official whereabouts.

PERSONNEL SECURITY

Today, reports abound that show associates. wife, grandchild, servants, and other blood relations who have arranged for the kidnap victims to acquire money. This myriad of threats shows that the procedure of threat calculation when done properly can be a bulky and complex effort. This is how bad insecurity presents its intimidation. Security preparedness is an important element in today's business environment which permits a business Executive the liberty to plan and perform his / her business strategies with minimum interference from the contestants and foes.

The Chief Executive Officer (CEO) of an organization is the life wire of the corporate body as the visionary of corporate operation. So any disaster or attack on the CEO portends great loss to the organization and will greatly affect corporate management. This is the reason the personal security of the CEO is important to corporate operations.

There are two types of threats in the commercial environment, direct and indirect. The direct method is when Business Executives face hostile surveillance activities and research that seek out proprietary information of other companies in order to stay competitive. It includes a systematic search of public information coupled with the aggressive collection and collation of competitive data through the internet, reverse engineering of products, manufacturing site inspection, and wide-ranging field interviews at trade fare exhibitions / events. Also, corporate information collected from unpublished Public Records; Statutory demands by administration agencies provide unnecessary information to competitors through the public domain.

The CEO and the family also face the threat of kidnapping for ransom and / or assassination.

The indirect threat can be evident in the form of unlawfully obtaining Information by overt and covert acts or causing or exploiting disloyalty and destroying or denying the use of vital material.

Decision-making also contends with economic espionage, Industrial Espionage, and Competitive Intelligence Professionals.

A corporate body is also vulnerable to Intentional acts; natural acts; accidental acts and environmental failures. These emergencies potentially call for organizations to put in place a security plan to protect and defend themselves against corporate / individual or natural mishaps.

The chief executive of an organization is its heartbeat and hub on which the company's performance hinges. therefore, he or she becomes a vulnerable target in the growing hostile economic environment. Business enterprises would need to have in place a layer of security protective measures for the chief executive to safeguard against crimes. Such includes ballistic resistance means being inserted in the executive's briefcase to deflect a handgun attack on the street and a ballistic resistant vest worn by the executive. The executive must become totally familiar with the environs and not develop a creature of habit. Doing the same thing at the same time and in the same place more than twice a week makes a person a creature of habit for this motive an executive should use different routes to and from work. If this is not possible, the executive should vary departure and arrival times by at least thirty minutes and identify a safe location to which an executive can go when being trailed. The executive should know how to recognize surveillance his / her family should be security conscious whilst the executive gives as little information as possible for local directories. The CEO should note choke points in his / her routes. Under no circumstances should an executive's home address or home telephone numbers be listed in directories. An executive should carefully select where and when to jog and should never jog alone.

The executive's vehicle must be kept in good condition and always have a fuel tank at least half full. The executive must always lock the car door and must wear his or her seat belt. The executive should always inform others where he or she is going and the estimated time of return, so delay can be checked. The executive should always give the vehicle a quick visual check before getting into it for any evidence of technical surveillance tampering. The executive should not touch suspicious objects but Install a car siren to alert people if the executive is being followed. The installation of interruption alarms is not so much for theft, but to prevent the placement of explosive devices or electronic trailers or transmitters. Such devices can also dissuade criminals.

ACQUIRING RESIDENCE FOR THE CEO

Residence remains one of the most vulnerable elements of protection that requires careful choice as it is not difficult for the criminal to find the resident in order to observe daily patterns of activities. And where to strike when the best opportunity presents itself. It is the personal responsibility of a high-profile individual to take sufficient security precautions, to ensure he / she no longer is an appealing target, and to make sure all members of his / her family are aware of security defenses.

Before purchasing / renting property, it is sensible to conduct a security audit. Security consultants may be hired to assist in this regard. The security audit should provide answers to the following insecurity indicators:

a. Is there too much vegetation too close to the house so that it makes concealment easy?

b. Where are the easy access points? How can these points be made secure?

c. Are there deadbolt locks on all outside doors?

d. Are there ways to observe a caller without opening the door and window locks?

e. Are there alternate exits, If there is somebody at one door?

f. How easy is it to escape through another door or through a window?

g. Is the property close to the security force station? How long will the reaction time be?

h. What about the neighbors?

i. How close are they?

j. Are the power, telephone, and utility lines protected, or can they be easily cut?

k. Is there an alarm system?

l. What is involved in the installation?

m. Who responds to the alarm?

n. Is there adequate outside lighting?

o. Does it come on automatically?

p. Is it on timers or sensors?

q. What about door locks?

r. The safest option is to change all locks before moving in and then to carefully keep track of who has keys.

When the house is eventually occupied, there are security disciplines that must be enforced such as:

a. Do not hand out keys to service people or workmen. If you lose your key, change the locks again.

b. Do not leave keys outside for neighbors or delivery people.

c. Making sure the home looks occupied at all times.

d. If the family is out for the evening, a radio or TV should be left playing.

e. When away for extended periods, a neighbor should visit daily to put out the garbage sweep walks, take in mail, or walk around the yard.

f. Anything to make it look like someone is there.

g. When the family returns after being away the executive should check the house carefully before entering.

h. If anyone looks suspicious, check with a neighbor or call the police. The family member should not let strangers in.

i. Several criminals use legitimate sounding ruses to gain entrance (auto breakdowns, sudden illness or accident, posing as service or delivery people).

j. Be on the lookout for cars or strangers that do not belong and take the license number or description in case it is necessary to report the incident to the police.

k. Keep the home secured at night by locking windows and doors.

l. The executive should be wary of telephone emergencies that require him or her to leave the house at odd hours.

m. Play it safe while verifying them with the appropriate authority. Everyone who has access to the house should have their background checked.

n. This includes babysitters, cleaning help, lawn persons, repair people, installers – anyone who has a chance to see what is inside or is in a position to have access, or who is in a position to "case the place" for future criminal activity.

o. In today's world, the potential exists for everyone to be burglarized.

p. Exercising caution can reduce the odds of that happening.

q. Always check references for all domestic help who will be in your home when you are not present. This includes a police check.

r. Keep a thorough data sheet on each employee.

s. Personal and financial records should be kept in a secured location. This includes cash and jewelry.

t. If workmen are performing a service at home, someone should be always nearby, even to the point of periodically checking to see how they are doing.

REFLEXION ON LOSS

u. Knowing that family members are on the alert reduces the opportunity for theft.

v. The resident should develop a complete inventory of all items at home. This can be done with a thorough list, a series of photographs of every room with a listing of all valuables, or a videotape documenting the possessions. U. And double-check this at regular intervals to make sure nothing is missing. Keep this record in a safe place away from the home, such as a bank security box.

w. Do not discuss finances or business matters in front of domestic help.

x. Be sure your domestic help, after they pass thorough security checks, are fully briefed on the family security procedures, how to answer the door and the phone, how to be on the lookout and report suspicious activity, and how to check identification of maintenance or service personnel. X. Keep retreat information confidential because knowing that the family is going to be away could be tempting to someone who sees it as a chance for easy money. Many homes have been robbed by what the owners believed was a "trusted" babysitter or cleaning person.

y. Do not allow domestic help to invite anyone into the home without your prior approval.

z. Keep the lending hand informed about specific times when you expect visitors, maintenance, and service personnel. Make certain the help understands how to properly check identification before the door is unlocked or opened.

aa. When an employee is dismissed or resigns, have your locks changed.

ab. Just as your family should vary its routine, so should house help. Shopping should be done at different times and / or on different days.

ac. Times and routes for the drop-off and pickup of children at school should vary as much as possible.

ad. Children should be taught certain things early in life, such as to avoid unnecessary contact with strangers and to withhold all personal information from them. They should learn to use the telephone to call for assistance. Tell them which neighbor to go to if they are threatened and remind them to be extra careful in opening doors to anyone they do not know.

ae. By age five, a child should be able to know his name, address, telephone number, and where his parents work. In addition, the following suggestions are for the self-protection of children. Children must travel in groups or pairs, walk along heavily traveled streets, and avoid isolated areas where possible. Refuse automobile rides from strangers and refuse to accompany strangers anywhere on foot. Never leave home without telling their parents where they will be and who will accompany them.

af. By the time children go to school, they spend increasingly more time away from the security of the home. Their greater exposure to the outside world increases their need for protection, but their safety depends on their own habits and resourcefulness. Children should do the same things adults do to increase their safety on the streets. They have legs to run with and voices to scream with when danger threatens.

ag. Encourage your children to tell you everything. If the child won't tell his parents about being picked on, robbed, or otherwise abused, then there's little they can do.

ah. Report every instance of crimes against your children to school authorities, and other parents and if sufficiently serious or repeated the police. If you are advised that your child has been bullying or robbing others, crack down hard. If a child gets away with stealing a pencil, it may be but a short step and a few years before he or she is ready to steal a car.

ai. It is sometimes a good idea for a child to learn karate, or some other forms of self-defense, especially if the child expresses an interest in these material arts. Even if he doesn't become accomplished enough really to defend himself, he will at least become self-confident, perhaps enough so to hurt a bully just once, which will generally be sufficient to gain immunity from further attack

aj. Children are probably never as troublesome as when they are in their teens. For parents, the first and most important protection for their teenager from crime, either as victim or criminal, know where their children are, what they are doing, and with whom. Your child is just as likely to be bad company as to be with bad company, and if you are too quick to spring to your offspring's defense, you may be an unwitting accomplice. Admit that your child could run foul of the law, and plan for this possibility with your teenager.

ak. Take him some time to see a jail if this can be arranged. Let him see what goes on inside. If you are willing to admit this responsibility, and you prepare him for it, perhaps he will be deterred. At least, keep the lines of communication open – they may help to head off teenage problems before they get too serious.

Teenage crime is often spawned in an atmosphere of poverty, hopelessness, drunkenness, squalor, frustration, idleness, and adult crime. It is a function of nobody-giving-a damn, especially parents, of school absenteeism and dropping out, and of peer group pressure.

al. Of the ingredients for spawning crime, only poverty seems to be an exclusive characteristic of the slum. The sub-urban juvenile delinquent is less deterred by possible consequences because he or she is much more likely to get off scot-free. Idleness is a problem as common in sub-urban as in the city. A part-time job is excellent for combating idleness and building self-confidence.

am. Open lines of communication between parents and children are wonderful, and although the teenage years are probably too late to start to establish these, you have nothing to lose and much to gain by trying. You need to make a teenager belong. If he doesn't feel he belongs at home, he will surely look for places and groups where he feels he does.

an. Make sure that outside doors, windows, and screens are security-locked before you retire at night. Be particularly certain that the child's room is not readily accessible from outdoors. If your home has an intercom system, leave the transmitter in a child's room open at night, or keep the door to the room open so that any usual noises may be heard. Since leaving the door open removes some fire protection, an intercom is better.

ao. Never leave young children at home alone or unattended and be certain they are left in the care of responsible trustworthy people. Children should learn early to keep the doors and windows locked and never to let in strangers. Teach children how to call for help if strangers or prowlers hang around the house or attempt to get in.

If you do leave the children at home for a short time, keep the house well-lighted and the garage doors shut. Instruct the household employees not to let in strangers or accept packages unless they are positive of the source.

REFLEXION ON LOSS

If you are expecting a package, alert household help to that fact.

ap. Kidnappers frequently have their victims under surveillance for several days prior to the kidnapping to acquaint themselves with the family's habits. Try to discourage your children from discussing family routines and remind yourself not to permit advance publicity from business trips or other occasions where you will be away from your home and family.

aq. Arrange for your children to be escorted to school and if you feel especially susceptible to kidnapping, do not let them take a taxi or public transportation.

ar. Beforehand releasing a child to anyone except his or her parents during the regular school day, an educator or administrative official should telephone one of the child's parents or guardians for approval. When a parent requests by phone that a child be released early from school, the caller's identity should be confirmed before the child is permitted to leave. If a parent is calling from home, the school should check the request by a return telephone call, with the child identifying the parent's voice. If the call is not being made from the child's house, the caller should be asked questions about such things as the child's date of birth, the courses he is studying, or the names of his educators and colleagues. If there is any doubt, the child should not be released.

as. Educators should be alert to suspicious-looking people who loiter in or near the school. If there is no logical explanation for their presence, the police should be notified immediately.

at. Everyone who has access to the residence should be checked. This includes babysitters, cleaning help, lawn persons, repair people, installers – anyone who has a chance to see what is inside, who can have access, or who can "case the home" for future criminal activity should be thoroughly vetted and vetted.

TIPS ON HIGHWAY DRIVING

There are no perfect security measures against crime on highways. A driver's best defense is training in surveillance and his power of alertness at all times. However, these few precautions are worthwhile as a strategy to safeguard against illegal attacks on highways.

If a driver suspects that a particular car has been following him or if he believes that a particular car has been too close behind his own vehicle in two or three places, he ought to watch out. It may be dangerous to allow such a car to overtake you; especially if it has young men in the front that is the driver and one other person or if the driver sits with a young woman in front and there is a third person at the back who appears to be sleeping. Generally, treat a car with that seating formation with the suspect.

Avoid potholes, they tend to slow one down and when you slow down in such dangerous areas, especially at night or in lonely areas, in the daytime criminals who hang around may splash engine oil content in black cellophane bags or raw eggs on the vehicle windscreen. Do not use your vehicle wipers at all as it will cause almost 99% poor visibility if you do and that will force you to stop. This is common in spots where crime thrives.

Watch out for cars close to or around the same point in opposite directions, sounding horns at the same time, or flashing their light at the same time. Suspicion should be increased if, in each of the two cars, there are two occupants. They may be on surveillance preparatory to an operation. But they may equally be innocent law-abiding people going on their legitimate business.

Another tactic is to hit the bumper of a targeted car to cleverly force the occupant to get out of the car for an agreement. The aim is to stop the car. When this happens and finds out that the offender is in a group of young men, it is safe to continue the journey, it may be fatal to be out of the car for an argument.

There is also the technique of using banger and knockout to scare people so that they abandon their cars. Note that the sound of a banger or knockout is different from that of a gun. In such a situation do not run away and abandon the car when you hear a sound. It may be a sound from a knockout.

Persons hanging around choke points and driving behind the target either when going out or coming into the house of the principal has been a common criminal tactic. However, the anti-dot is to look around to see if any car is following you as you are leaving or entering your home / office. If you suspect any, do not stop, drive ahead quickly turn to a nearby street, and continue the journey.

Chapter 8

Summary

The earth was created to be orderly, but mankind's wishes for power and wealth led to man's cruelty to mankind. This greed and self-centredness of a few individuals are evident in bad administration and governance with the resultant poor relations, lack of facilities, joblessness, crises, protests, capital flight, kidnapping, murder, armed burglary, and many other social evils.

The consequences of lawlessness affect everyone, the perpetrators of the erroneous character, employees / citizens, and the organization / nation. It is destructive in nature and manifestations which is always a time bomb. The spirit of procrastination in choice-making is evil and must be disheartened.

There are common difficulties with most administrative procedures. The first is that people wait too long before enforcing rewards and sanction systems. Many complaints and loss indicators do not receive a positive response from the authorities until there is a serious occurrence. Whereas many people wait until they have had serious security flout in advance to review worrisome procedures. The best approach is to expect misdeed in one form or another and then take necessary precautions to prevent it. Healthier to be safe than to be remorseful.

The second is that once the worrisome actions are reviewed, the propensity is to relax. This can major to laxity and it will never occur again position, which is the opportunity the mischief is looking for to prey targets.

Physical Security Procedures must be reviewed regularly. In the home, it can be as frequent as monthly.

It is particularly important to re-review the home's security at least twice a year. In the office, make unquestionable security procedures go over with all new departmental employees and establish a set of signals to be used in an emergency for the CEO. It can be set up between the CEO and the office and other family members and nearby neighbors.

Consider writing down all security rules for the home or office. It provides an excellent checklist when conducting periodic reviews.

CEOs should be careful about publicity. The efficacy of an executive security plan is heavily dependent on the executive's ability and willingness to maintain a low profile. Publicity in social columns or in connection with activities that call attention to possible prosperity, travel plans, club membership, and family status should be kept to a minimum. CEOs should use titles cautiously when in public places. Knowing he / she is a company representative may mark the CEO for a criminal attempt.

Take time to prepare a data sheet on each member of the CEO's domestic. This material serves as a ready reference in case of a kidnapping situation. In some circumstances, a company security division will want a tape of the executive's voice and the voices of domestic members for likely voice print purposes. Recent colored photos of family members are essential security records.

ABOUT THE AUTHOR

Sir Smart Odiase hails from the Uhunmwode local government area of Edo State and of the Emehi family in the Ohe N'isi community, Nigeria. His early life began at Ake Igbanke with his grandparents and subsequently Ohe with his parents. He attended the Nigerian Military School Zaria (NMS) from 1963 to 1967 passing out as the Boy Company Sergeant Major (BCSM) of the then Kaduna house, a school prefect, and a troop leader.

On completion of his military training in NMS, he was posted to the war front to join the Field Engineer Regiment and fought in the Nigerian Civil War (1967 - 1970) as a sapper tasked with the clearing of minefields laid by Biafra engineers. During the civil war, he was recommended to be commissioned as a combatant officer to the rank of 2nd Lieutenant in 1969.

Sir Smart's military career after the Civil War began as an intelligence officer. He was trained in various fields as an officer on deployment and management of infantry units. He attended several military courses home and abroad and distinguished himself in every aspect of training and military duties.

As an officer in the Nigerian Army Intelligence Corps (NAIC), he held many positions notably:

- Commander of the Intelligence and Security Group in the Nigerian Army Intelligence Corps (NAIC).
- Colonel Administration and Logistics.
- Colonel General Staff at the Directorate Military Intelligence (DMI).
- Director of Administration at the Special Investigation Panel (SIP) Supreme Headquarters.

- Deputy Director Intelligence at the Defence Intelligence Agency (DIA).

- Commandant Nigeria Army Intelligence School.

- Commandant State Security Service (SSS) Training School.

- Deputy Director Operations Defence Headquarters (DHQ).

Sir Smart retired from the Nigerian Army in 1990 as a Colonel after 30 years of faithful service to his country. He is happily married and blessed with children and grandchildren. He currently devotes his time in service to God as an ordained cleric passing on his life experiences and legacies. To God be the glory.

REFERENCES

1. Internet searches
2. Manual and program of ASIS
3. Security info watch
4. Holy Bible

Printed in Great Britain
by Amazon